the

STRANGEST
SECRET

Presented To:

_____

From:

_____

Date:

_____

Published and Distributed by

SOUND WISDOM
PO Box 310
Shippensburg, PA 17257-0310
717-530-2122

info@soundwisdom.com

www.soundwisdom.com

Cover design by Eileen Rockwell

ISBN 13 HC: 978-1-64095-106-8

ISBN 13 TP: 978-1-64095-108-2

ISBN 13 eBook: 978-1-64095-107-5

For Worldwide Distribution, Printed in the U.S.A.

HC - 1 2 3 4 5 6 / 21 20 19

TP - 6 7 8 9 10 11 / 25 24 23

Earl Nightingale

The key to success or failure is in your hands. What will you do with the Strangest Secret?

— *Earl Nightingale*

CONTENTS

PREFACE

Earl Nightingale (1921–1989) was a man of many talents and interests: a radio personality on a nationally syndicated show, an entrepreneur, a philosopher, a Marine, among other things. But one thread united all his pursuits—a passion for excellence and living a meaningful existence.

This passion drove him to seek out the secret formula for success. Accordingly, he spent his life studying the thoughts and habits of the select few in history who had achieved greatness in wealth and/or position, hoping to understand the difference between those who attain high levels of personal, professional, and financial success and those who do not.

While reading the line in Napoleon Hill's timeless classic *Think and Grow Rich* that "we become what we think about," Nightingale experienced his "Aha!" moment. The discovery that thoughts are things with very real effects—that having a concrete goal in your mind amounts to attaining it—fueled his success, enabling him to become financially independent by the time he was thirty-five.

Around the same time, Nightingale purchased an insurance company. He used his research into the laws of success to create weekly motivational speeches for his sales team. Because he was planning to be out of town during one of these speeches, he recorded a talk in advance to be played during his absence. His 1956 recording is one of the most inspiring speeches of all time, going on to become the first spoken word message to win a Gold Record by selling over a million copies.

In fact, demand for this recording became so great that Nightingale was encouraged to form, with the successful businessman Lloyd Conant, the "electronic publishing" company Nightingale-Conant, which has since become a multimillion-dollar giant in the personal development industry.

In his speech, what has since been titled *The Strangest Secret*, Nightingale distills his prodigious research on human motivation into a simple success formula that can be adopted by every individual, no matter his or her circumstances. According to Nightingale, the majority of the population ignores the importance of the Strangest Secret, instead languishing in a state of inactivity—aimless, dissatisfied, and lacking a sense of significance in life. This speech will teach you how to transform your

mindset so that you can become one of the top 5 percent who succeed in your field.

Toward the end of his speech, Nightingale details a thirty-day challenge for implementing the Strangest Secret. This test works to form new and healthy habits focused on goal achievement by helping you overcome toxic cycles of negative thinking. Self-doubt, worry, fear, and other negative emotions will undoubtedly hold you back in life. As the law of sowing and reaping indicates, if you plant these harmful emotions in the soil of your mind, you will harvest anxiety, fear, and failure. Your mind—and the universe more broadly—does not discriminate between positive and negative "crops": whether you sow poison or promise, you will reap that which you sow in equal measure. Once you replace limiting beliefs and negative thoughts with a calm, positive, and unswerving focus on a goal, you will trade emotional, spiritual, and financial poverty for abundance, and riches of all kinds will flow freely into your life.

The key to both success and failure is in your hands. What will you do with the Strangest Secret?

THE
STRANGEST
SECRET

Earl Nightingale

I'd like to tell you about the strangest secret in the world. Some years ago, the late Nobel Prize-winning Dr. Albert Schweitzer was being interviewed in London, and the reporter asked him, "Doctor, what's wrong with men today?"

The great doctor was silent a moment, and then he said, "Men simply don't think."

It's about this that I want to talk with you. We live today in a golden age. This is an era that man has looked forward to, dreamed of, and worked toward for thousands of years, but since it's here we pretty well take it for granted. We in America are particularly fortunate to live in the richest land that ever existed on the face of the earth—a land of abundant opportunity for everyone. But do you know what happens?

Let's take one hundred men to start, even at the age of twenty-five. Do you have any idea what will happen to those men by the time they're sixty-five? These one hundred men who all start even at the age of twenty-five believe they're going to be successful. If you ask any one of these men if he wanted to be a success, he'd tell you he did and you'd notice that he was eager toward life, that there was a certain sparkle to his eye, an erectness to his carriage, and life seemed like a pretty interesting adventure to him.

By the time they're sixty-five, one will be rich, four will be financially independent, five will still be working, fifty-four will be broke. Now, think a moment. Out of the one hundred, only five make the grade.

Now why do so many fail? What has happened to the sparkle that was there when they were twenty-five? What's become of the dreams, the hopes, the plans? And why is there such a large disparity between what these men intended to do and what they actually accomplished?

When we say about 5 percent achieve success, we have to define success, and here's the best definition I've ever been able to find: "Success is the progressive realization of a worthy ideal." If a man is working toward a predetermined goal and knows where he's going, that man is a success. If he's not doing that, he's a failure.

"Success is the progressive realization of a worthy ideal." Rollo May, the distinguished psychiatrist, wrote a wonderful book called *Man's Search for Himself*, and in his

SUCCESS

IS THE **PROGRESSIVE REALIZATION OF A WORTHY IDEAL.**

—Earl Nightingale

The success is the schoolteacher who's teaching school because that's what he or she wants to do. The success is the woman who's a wife and mother because she wanted to become a wife and mother and is doing a good job of it. The success is the man who runs the corner gas station because that was his dream, that's what he wanted to do. The success is the successful salesman who wants to become a top-notch salesman and grow and build with his organization. A success is anyone who is doing deliberately a predetermined job because that's what he decided to do deliberately.

— *Earl Nightingale*

book he says, "The opposite of courage in our society is not cowardice, it is conformity."

There you have the trouble today. It's conformity—people acting like everyone else without knowing why, without knowing where they're going.

Now think of it. In America right now, there are over eighteen million people sixty-five years of age and older. Most of them are broke. They're dependent on someone else for life's necessities.

We've learned to read by the time we're seven. We've learned to make a living by the time we're twenty-five. Usually by that time, we're not only making a living; we're supporting a family. And yet, by the time we're sixty-five, we haven't learned how to become financially independent in the richest land that has ever been known. Why?

We conform.

And the trouble is that we're acting like the wrong percentage group—the 95 who don't succeed.

Why do these people conform? Well, they really don't know. These people believe that their lives are shaped by circumstances, by things that happen to them, by exterior forces. They're outer-directed people.

A survey was made one time that covered a lot of men— working men—and these men were asked, "Why do you work? Why do you get up in the morning?" Nineteen out of twenty had no idea. If you ask a male, he'll say, "Everyone goes to work in the morning." And that's the reason they do it—because everyone else is doing it.

Now, let's get back to our definition of success. Who succeeds? The only person who succeeds is the person who is progressively realizing a worthy ideal. He's the person who says, "I'm going to become this" and begins to work toward that goal.

I'll tell you who the successful people are: The success is the schoolteacher who's teaching school because that's what he or she wants to do. The success is the woman who's a wife and mother because she wanted to become a wife and mother and is doing a good job of it. The success is the man

THE OPPOSITE | OF COURAGE

IN OUR SOCIETY IS NOT COWARDICE, IT IS CONFORMITY.

—Rollo May

We have a plateau of
so-called security
if that's what a
person's looking for,
but we do have to
decide how high above
this plateau we
want to aim.

—Earl Nightingale

who runs the corner gas station because that was his dream, that's what he wanted to do. The success is the successful salesman who wants to become a top-notch salesman and grow and build with his organization. A success is anyone who is doing deliberately a predetermined job because that's what he decided to do deliberately. But only one out of twenty does that.

That's why today there isn't any real competition, unless we make it for ourselves. Instead of competing, all we have to do is create. You know, for twenty years I looked for the key which would determine what would happen to a human being. Was there a key, I wanted to know, which would make the future a promise that we could foretell to a large extent? Was there a key that would guarantee a person's becoming successful if he only knew about it and knew how to use it?

Well, there is such a key, and I found it. Have you ever wondered why so many work so hard and honestly without ever achieving anything in particular and others don't seem to work hard and yet seem to get everything? They seem to have the magic touch. You've heard them say that about someone: "Everything he touches turns to gold."

Have you ever noticed that a man who becomes successful tends to continue to become successful? On the other hand, have you noticed how a man who's a failure tends to continue to fail?

Well, it's because of goals. Some of us have goals; some don't. People with goals succeed because they know where they're going. It's that simple.

Think of a ship leaving a harbor, and think of it with a complete voyage mapped out and planned. The captain and crew know exactly where it's going and how long it'll take. It has a definite goal. Now, 9,999 times out of 10,000 it will get to where it started out to get.

Let's take another ship just like the first, only let's not put a crew on it or a captain at a helm. Let's give it no aiming point, no goal, no destination. We just start the engines and let it go. I think you'll agree with me that if it gets out of the harbor at all, it'll either sink or wind up on some deserted beach, a derelict. It can't go any place because it has no destination and no guidance, and it's the same with a human being.

INSTEAD OF COMPETING, ALL WE HAVE TO DO IS CREATE.

—Earl Nightingale

If you understand completely what I'm going to tell you, from this moment on your life will never be the same again. You will suddenly find that good luck just seems to be attracted to you. The things you want just seem to fall in line, and from now on you won't have the problems, the worries, the gnawing lump of anxiety that perhaps you've experienced before. Doubt, fear—well, they will be things of the past.

— *Earl Nightingale*

Take a salesman, for example. There's no other person in the world today with the future of a good salesman. Selling is the world's highest paid profession if we're good at it and if we know where we're going. Every company needs top-notch salesmen, and they reward those men. The sky's the limit for them. But how many can you find?

Someone once said the human race is fixed, not to prevent the strong from winning, but to prevent the weak from losing. The American economy today can be likened to a convoy in a time of war. The entire economy is slowed down to protect its weakest link, just as the convoy had to go at the speed that would permit its slowest vessel to remain in formation.

That's why it's so easy to make a living today. It takes no particular brains or talent to make a living, to support a family today. We have a plateau of so-called security if that's what a person's looking for, but we do have to decide how high above this plateau we want to aim.

Now let's get back to the strangest secret in the world, the story that I wanted to tell you today. Why do men with goals succeed in life and men without them fail?

Well, let me tell you something which, if you really understand it, will alter your life immediately. If you understand completely what I'm going to tell you, from this moment on your life will never be the same again. You will suddenly find that good luck just seems to be attracted to you. The things you want just seem to fall in line, and from now on you won't have the problems, the worries, the gnawing lump of anxiety that perhaps you've experienced before. Doubt, fear—well, they will be things of the past.

Here's the key to success and the key to failure:

WE BECOME
what we think about.

Now, let me say that again: We become what we think about.

Throughout all history, the great wise men and teachers and philosophers and prophets have disagreed with one another on many different things. It's only on this one point that they are in complete and unanimous agreement.

A MAN'S LIFE IS WHAT HIS THOUGHTS MAKE OF IT.

—Marcus Aurelius

If you only care enough for a result, you will almost certainly attain it. If you wish to be rich, you will be rich. If you wish to be learned, you will be learned. If you wish to be good, you will be good. Only you must then really wish these things and wish them exclusively and not wish at the same time one hundred other incompatible things just as strongly.

—William James

Let's know what Marcus Aurelius, the great Roman emperor, said: "A man's life is what his thoughts make of it." Disraeli said this: "Everything comes if a man will only wait. I've brought myself by long meditation to the conviction that a human being with a subtle purpose must accomplish this and that nothing can resist a will that will stake even existence for its fulfillment."

Ralph Waldo Emerson said this: "A man is what he thinks about all day long."

William James said: "The greatest discovery of my generation is that human beings can alter their lives by altering their attitudes of mind." He also said: "We need only in cold blood act as if the thing in question were real and it will become infallibly real by growing into such a connection with our life that it will become real. It'll become so knit with habit and emotion that our interest in it will be those which characterize belief."

He also said: "If you only care enough for a result, you will almost certainly attain it. If you wish to be rich, you will be rich. If you wish to be learned, you will be learned. If you wish to be good, you will be good. Only you must then really wish these things and wish them exclusively and not wish at the same time one hundred other incompatible things just as strongly."

BELIEVE and **SUCCEED.**

In the Bible, you'll read in Mark 9:23: "If thou canst believe, all things are possible to him that believeth."

My old friend Dr. Norman Vincent Peale put it this way: "This is one of the greatest laws in the universe. Fervently do I wish I had discovered it as a very young man. It dawned upon me much later in life, and I have found it to be one of the greatest, if not my greatest, discovery outside of my relationship to God. The great law briefly and simply stated is that if you think in negative terms, you will get negative results. If you think in positive terms, you will achieve positive results. That is the simple fact," he went on to say, "which is at the basis of an astonishing law of prosperity and success." In three words: believe and succeed.

William Shakespeare put it this way: "Our doubts are traitors and make us lose the good we oft might win by fearing to attempt."

George Bernard Shaw said: "People are always blaming their circumstances for what they are. I don't believe in circumstances. The people who get on in this world are the people who get up and look for the circumstances they want and if they can't find them, make them."

Well, that is pretty apparent, isn't it? Every person who discovered this for a while believed that he was the first one to work it out. We become what we think about.

Now it stands to reason that a person who's thinking about a concrete and worthwhile goal is going to reach it because that's what he's thinking about. And we become what we think about.

Conversely, the man who has no goal, who doesn't know where he's going and whose thoughts must, therefore, be thoughts of confusion and anxiety and fear and worry, becomes what he thinks about. His life becomes one of frustration and fear and anxiety and worry. If he thinks about nothing, he becomes worried.

Now how does it work? Why do we become what we think about? Well, I'll tell you how it works, as far as I know. Now to do this, I want to tell you about a situation that parallels the human mind.

As ye sow,
SO SHALL YE REAP.

Suppose a farmer has some land and it's good, fertile land. Now the land gives the farmer a choice. He may plant in that land whatever he chooses. The land doesn't care. It's up to the farmer to make the decision.

Now remember, we're comparing the human mind with the land because the mind, like the land, doesn't care what you plant in it. It will return what you plant, but it doesn't care what you plant.

Now let's say that the farmer has two seeds in his hand. One is a seed of corn, the other is nightshade, a deadly poison. He digs two little holes in the earth, and he plants

both seeds—one corn, the other nightshade. He covers up the holes, waters and takes care of the land, and what will happen?

Invariably, the land will return what's planted. As it's written in the Bible, "As ye sow, so shall ye reap."

Now remember, the land doesn't care. It'll return poison in just as wonderful abundance as it will corn, so up come the two plants—one corn, one poison.

The human mind is far more fertile, far more incredible and mysterious, than the land, but it works the same way. It doesn't care what we plant—success, failure; a concrete, worthwhile goal or confusion, misunderstanding, fear, anxiety, and so on. But what we plant it must return to us.

You see, the human mind is the last great unexplored continent on earth. It contains riches beyond our wildest dreams. It will return anything we want to plant.

Now you might say, "Well, if that's true, why don't people use their minds more?" Well, I think they figured out an answer to that one too. Our mind comes as standard equipment at birth. It's free. And things that are given to us for nothing we place little value on. Things that we pay money for we value.

The paradox is that exactly the reverse is true. Everything that's really worthwhile in life came to us free. Our minds, our souls, our bodies, our hopes, our dreams, our ambitions, our intelligence, our love of family and children and friends and country—all these priceless possessions are free.

But the things that cost us money are actually very cheap and can be replaced at any time. A good man can be completely wiped out and make another fortune. He can do that several times. Even if our home burns down, we can rebuild it, but the things we got for nothing we can never replace.

The human mind isn't used because we take it for granted. Familiarity breeds contempt. The mind can do any kind of job we assign to it, but generally speaking we use it for little jobs instead of big ones. Universities have proven that most of us are operating at about 10 percent or less of our abilities.

A MAN

IS HE
WHAT

THINKS ABOUT
ALL DAY LONG.

—Ralph Waldo Emerson

Decide now: What is it you want? Plant your goal in your mind. It's the most important decision you'll ever make in your entire life.

— *Earl Nightingale*

The human mind is the last
great unexplored continent on earth.

Decide now: What is it you want? Plant your goal in your mind. It's the most important decision you'll ever make in your entire life.

What is it you want? Do you want to be an outstanding salesman? A better worker at your particular job? Do you want to go places in your company, in your community? Do you want to get rich? All you've got to do is plant that seed in your mind, care for it, work steadily toward your goal, and it will become a reality.

It not only will—there's no way that it cannot. You see, that's a law like the laws of Sir Isaac Newton, the laws of gravity. If you get on top of a building and jump off, you'll always go down; you'll never go up. And it's the same with all the other laws of nature: they always work; they're inflexible.

Think about your goal in a relaxed, positive way. Picture yourself in your mind's eye as having already achieved this goal. See yourself doing the things you will be doing when you've reached your goal.

Ours has been called the phenobarbital age, the age of ulcers and nervous breakdowns and tranquilizers. At a time when medical research has raised us to a new plateau of good health and longevity, far too many of us worry ourselves into an early grave trying to cope with things in our own little personal ways without learning a few great laws that will take care of everything for us.

These things we bring on ourselves through our habitual way of thinking. Every one of us is the sum total of his own thoughts. He is where he is because that's exactly where he really wants to be, whether he'll admit that or not. Each of us must live off the fruit of his thoughts in the future, because what you think today and tomorrow, next month and next year, will mold your life and determine your future. You're guided by your mind.

PLANT YOUR GOAL IN YOUR MIND.

PICTURE YOUR-SELF IN YOUR MIND'S EYE AS HAVING ALREADY ACHIEVED THIS GOAL.

—Earl Nightingale

What you think today and tomorrow, next month and next year, will mold your life and determine your future.

— Earl Nightingale

I remember one time I was driving through eastern Arizona, and I saw one of those giant earth-moving machines roaring along the road at about thirty-five miles an hour with what looked like thirty tons of dirt in it—a tremendous, incredible machine. There was a little man perched way up on top with the wheel in his hands, guiding it.

As I drove along, I was struck by the similarity of that machine to the human mind. Just suppose you're sitting at the controls of such a vast source of energy. Are you going to sit back and fold your arms and let it run itself into a ditch? Or are you going to keep both hands firmly on the wheel and control and direct this power to a specific, worthwhile purpose? It's up to you. You're in the driver's seat.

You see, the very law that gives us success is a two-edged sword. We must control our thinking. The same rule that can lead a man to a life of success, wealth, happiness, and all the things he ever dreamed of for himself and his family, that very same law can lead him into the gutter. It's all in how he uses it, for good or for bad. That is the strangest secret in the world.

Now, why do I say it's strange, and why do I call it a secret? Actually, it isn't a secret at all. It was first promulgated by some of the earliest wise men, and it appears again and again throughout the Bible. But very few people have learned it or understand it. That's why it's strange and why, for some equally strange reason, it virtually remains a secret.

I believe that you could go out and walk down the main street of your town and ask one man after another what the secret of success is, and you probably wouldn't run into one man in a month who could tell you.

Now, this information is enormously valuable to us if we really understand it and apply it. It's valuable to us not only for our own lives but the lives of those around us— our families, employees, associates, and friends. Life should be an exciting adventure. It should never be a bore. A man should live fully, be alive. He should be glad to get out of bed in the morning. He should be doing a job he likes to do because he does it well.

One time I heard Grove Patterson, the great late editor-in-chief of *The Toledo Blade*, make a speech, and as he concluded his speech he said something I've never

THE GREATEST DISCOVERY OF MY GENERATION IS THAT HUMAN BEINGS CAN ALTER THEIR LIVES BY ALTERING THEIR ATTITUDES OF MIND.

—William James

Life should be an
exciting adventure.
It should never be a
bore. A man should
live fully, be alive.

—Earl Nightingale

forgotten. He said, "My years in the newspaper business have convinced me of several things, among them that people are basically good and that we came from someplace and we're going someplace, so we should make our time here an exciting adventure. The architect of the universe didn't build a stairway leading nowhere."

The greatest teacher of all, the carpenter from the plains of Galilee, gave us the secret time and time again: "As ye believe, so shall it be done unto you."

I've explained the strangest secret in the world and how it works. Now I want to explain how you can prove to yourself the enormous returns possible in your own life by putting the secret to a practical test. I want you to make a test that will last thirty days. It isn't going to be easy, but if you give it a good try, it will completely change your life for the better.

Back in the seventeenth century, Sir Isaac Newton, the English mathematician and natural philosopher, gave

No matter what your present job, it has enormous possibilities if you're willing to pay the price.

— Earl Nightingale

us the natural laws of physics, which apply as much to human beings as they do to the movement of bodies in the universe. One of these laws is that for every action, there is an equal and opposite reaction. Simply stated as it applies to you and me, it means that we can achieve nothing without paying the price.

The results of your thirty-day experiment will be in direct proportion to the effort you put forth. To be a doctor, you must pay the price of long years of difficult study. To be successful in selling—and remember that each of us succeeds to the extent of his ability to sell: selling our families on our ideas, selling education in schools, selling our children on the advantages of living the good and honest life, selling our associates and employees on the importance of being exceptional people, and of course, the profession of selling itself—to be successful in selling our way to the good life, we must be willing to pay the price.

Now, what is that price? Well, it's many things.

First, it's understanding emotionally as well as intellectually that we literally become what we think about, that we must control our thoughts if we are to control our lives. It's understanding fully that as ye sow, so shall ye reap.

Second, it's cutting away all fetters from the mind and permitting it to soar as it was divinely designed to do. It's the realization that your limitations are self-imposed and that the opportunities for you today are enormous beyond belief. It's rising above narrowminded pettiness and prejudice.

Third, it's using all your courage to...

...force yourself to think positively on your own problem,

...set a definite and clearly defined goal for yourself and let your marvelous mind think about your goal from all possible angles,

...let your imagination speculate freely upon many different possible solutions,

...refuse to believe that there are any circumstances sufficiently strong enough to defeat you in the accomplishment of your purpose,

...act promptly and decisively when your course is clear and to keep constantly aware of the fact that you are, at this moment, standing in the middle of your own "acres of diamonds," as Russell Conwell used to point out.

Fourth, save at least 10 percent of every dollar you earn.

It's also remembering that no matter what your present job, it has enormous possibilities if you're willing to pay the price.

The Price of **Success**

1. Understanding that thoughts are things and that you must control your thoughts in order to control your life.

2. Realizing that limitations are self-imposed and that you must cut yourself free from them.

3. Summoning all your courage to:

   - Think positively on your problem
   - Establish a definite goal
   - Allow your imagination to creatively reflect on various possible solutions

- Act promptly and decisively when your course is clear

4. Saving at least 10 percent of your earnings.

5. Remembering that no matter what your present job, it has enormous possibilities if you're willing to pay the price.

Now, let's just go over the important points and the price each of us must pay to achieve the wonderful life that can be ours. It is, of course, worth any price.

- You will become what you think about.

- Remember the word "imagination," and let your mind begin to soar.

- Courage—concentrate on your goal every day.

- Save 10 percent of what you earn.

- Action—ideas are worthless unless we act on them.

Now I'll try to outline the thirty-day test I want you to take. Keep in mind that you have nothing to lose by making this test and everything you could possibly want to gain.

There are two things that may be said of everyone: each of us wants something, and each of us is afraid of something.

I want you to write on a card what it is you want more than anything else. It may be more money. Perhaps you'd like to double your income or make a specific amount of money. It may be a beautiful home. It may be success at your job. It may be a particular position in life. It could be a more harmonious family.

Each of us wants something. Write down on your card specifically what it is you want. Make sure it's a single goal and clearly defined. You needn't show it to anyone, but carry it with you so that you can look at it several times a day. Think about it in a cheerful, relaxed, positive way each morning when you get up, and immediately you have something to work for, something to get out of bed for, something to live for.

Look at it every chance you get during the day and just before going to bed at night. As you look at it, remember

Your goal is yours the moment you write it down and begin to think about it.

— *Earl Nightingale*

that you must become what you think about, and since you're thinking about your goal, you realize that soon it will be yours. In fact, it's yours, really, the moment you write it down and begin to think about it.

Look at the abundance all around you as you go about your daily business. You have as much right to this abundance as any other living creature. It's yours for the asking.

Now we come to the difficult part—difficult because it means the formation of what is probably a brand-new habit. New habits are not easily formed. Once formed, however, it'll follow you for the rest of your life.

Stop thinking about what it is you fear. Each time a fearful or negative thought comes into your consciousness, replace it with a mental picture of your positive and worthwhile goal. There will come times when you'll feel like giving up. It's easier for a human being to think negatively than positively. That's why only 5 percent are successful. You must begin now to place yourself in that group.

For thirty days, you must take control of your mind. It will think about only what you permit it to think about.

Ask, and it shall be given you; seek, and ye shall find; knock, and it shall be opened unto you. For every one that asketh receiveth; and he that seeketh findeth; and to him that knocketh it shall be opened. (Matthew 7:7–8 KJV)

Each day for this thirty-day test, do more than you have to do. In addition to maintaining a cheerful, positive outlook, give of yourself more than you've ever done before. Do this knowing that your returns in life must be in direct proportion to what you give.

The moment you decide on a goal to work toward, you're immediately a successful person. You are then in that rare and successful category of people who know where they're going. Out of every one hundred people, you belong to the top five.

Don't concern yourself too much with how you're going to achieve your goal. Leave that completely to a power greater than yourself. All you have to know is where you're going. The answers will come to you of their own accord and at the right time.

Remember these words from the Sermon on the Mount, and remember them well. Keep them constantly before you this month of your test:

> *Ask, and it shall be given you; seek, and ye shall find; knock, and it shall be opened unto you. For every one that asketh receiveth; and*

Your returns in life must be in direct proportion to what you give.

— *Earl Nightingale*

*he that seeketh findeth; and to him that knock-
eth it shall be opened.*

It's as marvelous and as simple as that. In fact, it's so simple that in our seemingly complicated world, it's difficult for an adult to understand that all they need is a purpose and faith.

For thirty days, do your very best. If you're a salesman, go at it as you have never done before—not in a hectic fashion, but with the calm, cheerful assurance that time well spent will give you the abundance in return that you want.

If you're a homemaker, devote your thirty-day test to completely giving of yourself without thinking about receiving anything in return, and you will be amazed at the difference it makes in your life.

No matter what your job, do it as you've never done before for thirty days. And if you have kept your goal before you every day, you'll wonder and marvel at this new life you have found.

Dorothea Brande, the outstanding editor and writer, discovered it for herself and talks about it in her fine book

Wake up and Live! Her entire philosophy is reduced to the words: "Act as though it were impossible to fail." She made her own test with sincerity and faith, and her entire life was changed to one of overwhelming success.

Now, you make your test for thirty full days. Don't start your test until you have made up your mind to stick with it. You see, by being persistent, you're demonstrating faith. Persistence is simply another word for faith. If you didn't have faith, you'd never persist.

If you should fail during your first thirty days—by that I mean finding suddenly yourself overwhelmed by negative thoughts—you've got to start over again from that point and go thirty more days.

Gradually, your new habit will form, until you find yourself one of that wonderful minority to whom virtually nothing is impossible.

And don't forget the card! It's vitally important as you begin this new way of living. On one side of the card, write your goal, whatever it may be. On the other side, write the words we've quoted from the Sermon on the Mount: "Ask,

ACT AS IT WERE **IMPOSSIBLE** THOUGH TO FAIL.

—Dorothea Brande

Be of service. Build, work, dream, create. Do this, and you'll find there's no limit to the prosperity and abundance that will come to you.

— *Earl Nightingale*

and it shall be given you; seek, and ye shall find; knock, and it shall be opened unto you."

Nothing great was ever accomplished without inspiration. See that during these crucial first thirty days your own inspiration is kept at a peak.

Above all, don't worry. Worry brings fear, and fear is crippling. The only thing that can cause you to worry during your test is trying to do it all yourself.

Know that all you have to do is hold your goal before you. Everything else will take care of itself.

Remember also to keep calm and cheerful. Don't let petty things annoy you and get you off course.

Now, since making this test is difficult, some will say, "Why should I bother?" Well, look at the alternative. No one wants to be a failure. No one really wants to be a mediocre individual. No one wants a life constantly filled with worry and fear and frustration.

Therefore, remember that you must reap that which you sow. If you sow negative thoughts, your life will be filled with negative things. If you sow positive thoughts, your life will be cheerful, successful, and positive.

Now, gradually you will have a tendency to forget what you've heard on this recording. Play it often. Keep reminding yourself of what you must do to form this new habit. Gather your whole family around at regular intervals and listen to what's been said here.

Most men will tell you that they want to make money, without understanding the law. The only people who "make money" work in a mint. The rest of us must earn money. This is what causes those who keep looking for something for nothing, or a free ride, to fail in life.

The only way to earn money is by providing people with services or products which are needed and useful. We exchange our time and our product or service for the other man's money. Therefore, the law is that our financial return will be in direct proportion to our service.

Now, success is not the result of making money. Earning money is the result of success, and success is in direct proportion to our service. Most people have this law backward. They believe that you are successful if you earn

a lot of money. The truth is that you can only earn money after you are successful.

It's like the story of the man who sat in front of the stove and said to it: "Give me heat, and then I'll add the wood."

How many men and women do you know, or do you suppose there are today, who take the same attitude toward life? There are millions. We've got to put the fuel in before we can expect heat. Likewise, we've got to be of service first before we can expect money.

Don't concern yourself with the money. Be of service. Build, work, dream, create. Do this, and you'll find there's no limit to the prosperity and abundance that will come to you.

Prosperity is founded upon a law of mutual exchange. Any person who contributes to prosperity must prosper in turn himself.

Sometimes the return will not come from those you serve, but it must come to you from someplace because that's the law. For every action, there is an equal and opposite reaction.

As you go daily through your thirty-day test period, remember that your success will always be measured by the quality and quantity of service you render, and money is a yardstick for measuring this service. No man can get rich himself unless he enriches others. Now, there are no exceptions to a law.

You can drive down any street in America and from your car estimate the service that's being rendered by the people living on that street. Have you ever thought of this yardstick before? It's interesting. Some, like ministers and priests and other devoted people, measure their returns in the realm of the spiritual, but again their returns are equal to their service.

Once this law is fully understood, any thinking person can tell his own fortune. If he wants more, he must be of more service to those from whom he receives his return. If he wants less, he has only to reduce his service. This is the price you must pay for what you want.

If you believe you can enrich yourself by deluding others, you can end only by deluding yourself. It may take some time, but just as surely as you breathe, you'll get back

THE FORCE BEHIND EVERY HUMAN ACTION IS ITS GOAL.

—Earl Nightingale

No man can get rich himself unless he enriches others.

—*Earl Nightingale*

what you put out. Don't ever make the mistake of thinking you can avert this. It's impossible.

The prisons and the streets where the lonely walk are filled with people who tried to make new laws just for themselves. We may avoid the laws of man for a while, but there are greater laws that cannot be broken.

An outstanding medical doctor recently pointed out six steps that will help you realize success:

1. Set yourself a definite goal.

2. Quit running yourself down.

3. Stop thinking of all the reasons why you cannot be successful and instead think of all the reasons why you can.

4. Trace your attitudes back to your childhood and try to discover where you first got the idea that you couldn't be successful if that's the way you've been thinking.

5. Change the image you have of yourself by writing out a description of the person you would like to be.

6. Act the part of the successful person you have decided to become.

The doctor who wrote those words is a noted West Coast psychiatrist, Dr. David Harold Fink.

Do what the experts since the dawn of recorded history have said you must do: pay the price by becoming the person you want to become. It's not nearly as difficult as living unsuccessfully.

Make your thirty-day test, then repeat it, then repeat it again. Each time it will become more a part of you, until you'll wonder how you could have ever have lived any other way.

Live this new way, and the floodgates of abundance will open and pour over you more riches than you may have dreamed existed.

Money? Yes, lots of it—but what's more important, you'll have peace. You'll be in that wonderful minority who lead calm, cheerful, successful lives.

Start today. You have nothing to lose, but you have a whole life to win.

EARL NIGHTINGALE'S
30-DAY CHALLENGE

Nightingale's famous thirty-day test has transformed the mindsets—*and lives*—of countless people across the globe, giving them phenomenal levels of financial and professional success, as well as the ultimate form of wealth—an abiding, deep-rooted *joy of life.*

Now it's your turn to implement this life-changing challenge. In thirty days, you will discover more abundance than you could ever have imagined—likely monetary riches, but more importantly, emotional riches like serenity, satisfaction, and gratitude. While the test lasts only a month, it should be repeated again and again until it becomes a part of you.

Nightingale's challenge addresses two facets of the human condition: our core desires as well as our basic fears. As he says, "Each of us wants something, and each of us is afraid of something." This reality undergirds his philosophy of individual achievement, which is grounded in the science of the mind—namely, the notion that thoughts are things, and when you change your thoughts, you change your reality.

Accordingly, the thirty-day test recommends actions that will turn your innermost desire into a concrete goal and your nagging fears into a new, productive habit. It involves two ongoing processes:

1. Goal-making

- Write on a card what it is you want more than anything else—a single, clearly defined goal.

- On the other side, write the following lines from the Sermon on the Mount:

Ask, and it shall be given you; seek, and ye shall find; knock, and it shall be opened unto you. For every one that asketh receiveth; and he that seeketh findeth; and to him that knock-eth it shall be opened.

—Matthew 7:7–8 KJV

- Carry this card with you at all times, and periodically take it out and read both sides. Make sure to remain positive about your goal. As Nightingale instructs, "Think about it in a cheerful, relaxed way." He further advises: "As

you look at it, remember that you must become
what you think about, and since you're thinking
about your goal, you realize that soon it will be
yours."

2. New habit formation

- The second component of the test involves
  refraining from thinking about your fears—
  because the rule that "you become what you
  think about" applies just as much to negative
  thoughts as it does to positive ones.

- Nightingale instructs: "Each time a fearful or
  negative thought comes into your consciousness, replace it with a mental picture of your
  positive and worthwhile goal."

These two activities—remaining focused on your most
desired goal and not succumbing to intrusive negative
thoughts—are inherently intertwined. The idea is to
maintain a cheerful, relaxed, positive outlook on life while
intensively pursuing your dreams. Doing so will not only
ensure that you reach your goals; it will also guarantee

your enjoyment of the process—because as Nightingale repeatedly emphasizes throughout his work, having goals are what give life meaning.

His first rule of living is that "a human being must have something worthwhile toward which he's working. Without that, everything else—even the most remarkable achievements and all the trappings of worldly success— tend to turn sour." Nightingale adds: "The moment you decide on a goal to work toward, you're immediately a successful person." For him, the journey of pursuing your goals is just as important, if not more important, than the attainment of them. And riches can be found in both the process and the product.

In addition to maintaining a cheerful, positive outlook while reflecting on and taking action to reach your goal, Nightingale recommends giving of yourself more than you've ever done before. Work harder at your job than you ever have. Take on extra tasks with a positive attitude, and do your regular duties with a keener eye for detail and commitment to excellence than usual. Add value before expecting returns to manifest, and value will be added unto you. The law of giving and receiving, of sowing and

reaping, ensures that you will receive in equal measure that which you contribute: poison for poison, or bounty for bounty; failure for toxic, negative thoughts, or success for positive, peaceful thoughts. In other words, emit thoughts with positive frequencies that will yield a generous harvest of riches.

Note that if at any point in the thirty days, you vocalize a negative thought, you must start over again from that point and go thirty more days.

STARTING YOUR 30-DAY TEST

In order to begin your thirty-day challenge, you must decide upon a concrete goal to pursue. Nightingale recommends that you choose only one to focus on for this particular test, so you'll have to identify your most desired objective.

Nightingale provides the following questions to help you determine what it is you truly want in life:

1. If you could completely change places with any other person in the world, would you do it, and who would that person be?

_____

_____

_____

2. If you could work at any job, would that work be different from the work you're doing now?

_____

_____

_____

3. If you could live in any part of the country, would you move from where you're now living, and if so, where?

_____

_____

4. If you could go back to age twelve and live your life from that point over again, would you do it? And what would you do differently?

_____

_____

Nightingale notes that most people will answer "no" to all four questions, even when they're generally dissatisfied with their present lives—which, in his mind, explains their unhappiness. For goals are what give our lives purpose and direction.

Go ahead and think critically upon each one of these questions. Journal about your responses, exploring not only the *who*, *what*, *where*, and *how* questions implied in prompts 1–4, but also the *whys*:

1. If you would change places with someone, why that particular person? What is it about his or her life that you would like to emulate? Can you identify in one sentence, or even one phrase, what that person has that you desire?

_____

_____

_____

_____

_____

2. If you would choose a different profession, why that specific career? What qualities about that career make it desirable to you? Are any of these qualities present in your current job that could be further developed? What is your most desired job title and why?

_____

_____

_____

_____

_____

3. If you would like to move to a different location, why that particular location? What aspects of that location make it ideal for your home? Are any of these qualities present in other locations, including your current one? Or, do you simply desire a different home in the same general location?

_____

_____

_____

_____

_____

_____

_____

_____

_____

_____

_____

_____

4. Why would doing that particular thing in your life over again differently make a difference? What was it about that action or event that you didn't like? What were its consequences? Why would the alternate scenario you imagined in the above prompt have produced better results?

_____

_____

_____

_____

_____

_____

_____

_____

_____

_____

_____

_____

Based on your answers to these questions, rank, on a scale of 1 to 6 (1 being most desired and 6 being least desired), the areas of your life in which you most desire change:

- [ ] Wellness
- [ ] Finances
- [ ] Career
- [ ] Location
- [ ] Personality
- [ ] Relationships

After selecting the department of living upon which you'll focus your thirty-day test from the list above, find the correlating prompt below to help write your concrete goal statement on the front side of your reminder card.

Remember, your goal statement should be **one concise sentence** that clearly defines a **specific** goal. Use one or more of the questions in the category of your choice to formulate your unique goal statement.

Eare Westright

WELLNESS

1. How do you define "health" or "wellness"?

   _____

   _____

   _____

   _____

2. If you imagine yourself living at a peak level of wellness,
   what does that involve?

   _____

   _____

   _____

   _____

3. How does your current lifestyle differ from the lifestyle required for your ideal state of wellness?

4. What are you willing to sacrifice to reach your wellness goal?

— SAMPLE GOAL STATEMENTS —

I desire increased health/wellness in my life, which entails _____.

In _____ [years/months], I would like to _____ [lose ____ pounds; take up _____ sport or mindfulness regimen; transition into veganism; etc.].

FINANCES

1. What is the salary that would make you content, comfortable, or overjoyed? Write an exact number.

   _____

2. Do you have any debt that you would like cleared? How much does this debt amount to? In how many years would you like to pay off this balance? How will you feel when you clear this debt?

   _____

   _____

   _____

   _____

3. How much money would you like to contribute to savings each month? Or what other investments would you like to make?

_____

_____

_____

_____

4. What large item would you like to purchase? How much is required for you to purchase this item?

_____

_____

5. How much money would you like to give annually or monthly to philanthropic purposes? To what causes would you contribute your funds? Why do you value these causes?

_____

_____

_____

_____

6. What are you willing to give up to reach your financial goal?

_____

_____

_____

_____

— SAMPLE GOAL STATEMENTS —

In _____ years, I would like to make
_____ and be able to
contribute _____ annually to charities like
_____ and _____.

In _____ years, I would like to pay off _____
in debt and be making _____ per year.

I will forgo _____ [miscellaneous
expense] in order to save an extra _____
per month.

I will save _____ each month in order to
buy _____ in _____ [years/months].

CAREER

1. What is your dream job and why? Include the specific job title in your description.

_____

_____

_____

_____

2. Is there a different role in your current company that you would rather have? If so, what? Write the specific job title.

_____

_____

_____

_____

3. Do you desire to start your own business? If so, what kind? Why do you value entrepreneurship?

_____

_____

_____

_____

_____

4. If your dream job is in a different field than your current one, what education or training will be required for you to change professions? Or who could mentor you in your desired industry?

_____

_____

_____

_____

_____

5. In how many years would you like to make this job change?

   _____

6. What are you willing to sacrifice to reach your professional goal?

   _____

   _____

   _____

   _____

   _____

— Sample Goal Statements —

In _____ years, I would like to be the
_____ at my current company.

In _____ years, I would like to start my own
_____ company because
_____.

In _____ years, I would like to switch professions
to _____, which means that I'll need
to seek training in _____.

LOCATION

1. Where in the world would you most like to live and why?

   _____

   _____

   _____

   _____

   _____

2. Can you do your current job in this location, or would you need to change careers? What else would be required to move to this other place?

   _____

   _____

   _____

   _____

   _____

3. In what type of home would you most like to live? Describe the specific home type (Cape Cod, colonial, craftsman, etc.; two-story, ranch, split-level, etc.; brick, stucco, etc.) in as much detail as possible.

_____

_____

_____

_____

_____

4. What are you willing to give up to live in this location?

_____

_____

_____

_____

_____

— SAMPLE GOAL STATEMENTS —

In _____ [years/months], I would like to live in

_____ .

In _____ [years/months], I will move into a

_____ style house in _____ [location].

Eric Wright

PERSONALITY

1. What are the qualities in other people I most like? Which of these qualities could I do better to cultivate?

   _____

   _____

2. What personality characteristics would most lend themselves to a happier, more cheerful, more relaxed life?

   _____

   _____

3. What am I willing to change about my current life to adopt a more pleasing (both to self and to others) personality?

   _____

   _____

— SAMPLE GOAL STATEMENTS —

I intend to become a better version of myself,
which involves cultivating the following personality
characteristics:

_____

_____

_____

_____

Every day, I will remain calm, positive, and grateful,
approaching each challenge as an opportunity for
growth and success.

Eckhart Tolle

RELATIONSHIPS

1. How could my current relationships be improved?

   _____

   _____

   _____

   _____

   _____

2. What relationships are currently absent from my life
   that I would like to cultivate?

   _____

   _____

   _____

   _____

   _____

3. What am I willing to sacrifice to develop, repair, or improve these relationships?

_____

_____

_____

_____

_____

— SAMPLE GOAL STATEMENTS —

In _____ [years/months], I will find my future [spouse/partner] by _____.

In _____ [years/months], I will strengthen my relationship with _____, which will require _____.

**Start today.
You have nothing to
lose—but you have
your whole life
to win.**

—Eave Wright